small worlds

A CORAL REEF

Jen Green

CRABTREE
Publishing Company
www.crabtreebooks.com

Crabtree Publishing Company

www.crabtreebooks.com

PMB 16A, 350 Fifth Avenue
Suite 3308
New York, NY 10118

612 Welland Avenue
St. Catharines
Ontario L2M 5V6

CRABTREE:
Project editor: P. A. Finlay
Assistant editor: Carrie Gleason
Coordinating editor: Ellen Rodger

BROWN PARTWORKS:
Editor: Amanda Harman
Designer: Joan Curtis
Picture researcher: Clare Newman
Managing editor: Bridget Giles
Commissioning editor: Anne O'Daly
Consultants: Gary C. Williams, PhD, Curator of Coelenterates, Department of Invertebrate Biology, California Academy of Sciences, and J. C. Lewis, PhD

Illustrator: Peter Bull

Photographs: Jeff Foot/Bruce Coleman Collection p 16*m*; Jim Watt/Bruce Coleman Collection p 24*m*; Stephen Frink/Corbis front and back covers, pp 3, 5, 8*t*, 9, 10, 11, 12*t*, 12*b*, 16*t*, 17, 19, 21, 24*t*, 30; Catherine Karnow/Corbis p 28; Amos Nachoum/Corbis pp 4, 6; Phil Schermeister/Corbis p 31; Stuart Westmorland pp 14, 25; Lawson Wood/ Corbis pp 27*t*, 27*b*; B. Jones and M. Shimlock/NHPA p 20*b/r*; Trevor McDonald/NHPA pp 7*b*, 13; Norbert Wu/NHPA title page, pp 7*t*, 18, 20*b/l*, 23; Brent Deuel/NOAA p 8*m*.

Created and produced by
Brown Partworks Limited

First edition
10 9 8 7 6 5 4 3 2 1
Copyright © 2002 Brown Partworks Limited
Printed in Singapore

CATALOGING-IN-PUBLICATION DATA

Green, Jen.
  A coral reef / Jen Green.-- 1st ed.
  p. cm. -- (Small worlds)
  Summary: Provides an introduction to the world's coral reefs, as well as the thousands of sea creatures that live there.
  ISBN 0-7787-0138-7 (RLB) -- ISBN 0-7787-0152-2 (pbk.)
  1. Coral reef animals--Juvenile literature. 2. Coral reefs and islands--Juvenile literature. [1. Coral reef animals. 2. Coral reefs and islands.] I. Title II. Small worlds (New York, N.Y).
  QL125 .G73 2002
  591.77'89--dc21
                          2001042420
                          LC

Contents

Reefs around the world   4

Life on the reef   6

The coral kingdom   8

Bright colors, amazing shapes   16

Predators and prey   24

Getting to know reefs   30

Words to know   32

Index   32

Reefs around the world

The clear blue waters of many warm shallow seas around the world are home to coral reefs, one of nature's wonders.

Sponges, such as this rope sponge, are common on coral reefs. Some look similar to the corals themselves.

The magical underwater gardens of coral reefs support thousands of colorful sea animals. Some reefs are giant rocky structures that rise through the water like towering skyscrapers. The largest reefs are so big they can be seen from space—yet they are built by animals called **polyps**, which are often smaller than peas.

This book will introduce you to some of the strange and beautiful animals that live on coral reefs around the world.

Some parts of the world have many coral reefs. There are more than 50 coral reefs in the Florida Keys region alone.

Most of the world's coral reefs are located in the tropics, the warm regions of the Earth either side of the equator (dotted line).

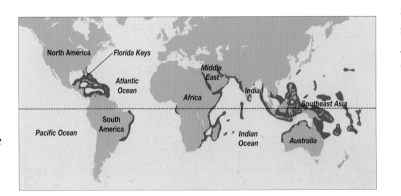

North America — Florida Keys — Atlantic Ocean — Middle East — India — Africa — Southeast Asia — Pacific Ocean — South America — Indian Ocean — Australia

Life on the reef

Coral reefs are similar to tropical rainforests because both are full of life. Nearly one-quarter of all ocean *species* live on or around coral reefs.

remora

shark

barracuda

shark

moray eel

Reef-building corals can only live in sunlit shallow waters that stay warm all year. Fringe reefs form off coasts and islands; barrier reefs also occur along coasts but lie farther out to sea. Atolls are circular reefs around sunken islands.

Coral reefs can be divided into zones. In each zone, the amount of sunlight that reaches through the water and the temperature varies. Each part of the reef has a different set of animals that thrives there.

The coral kingdom
Tiny animals called coral polyps build the reef. Sea anemones and sponges attach themselves to the rocky surface. Thousands of small sea animals, including shrimp, crabs, and sea urchins, live on and around the reef.

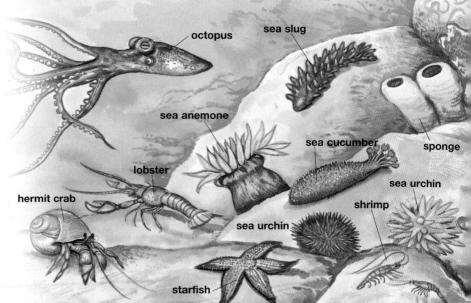

octopus

sea slug

sea anemone

sea cucumber

sponge

lobster

sea urchin

shrimp

hermit crab

sea urchin

starfish

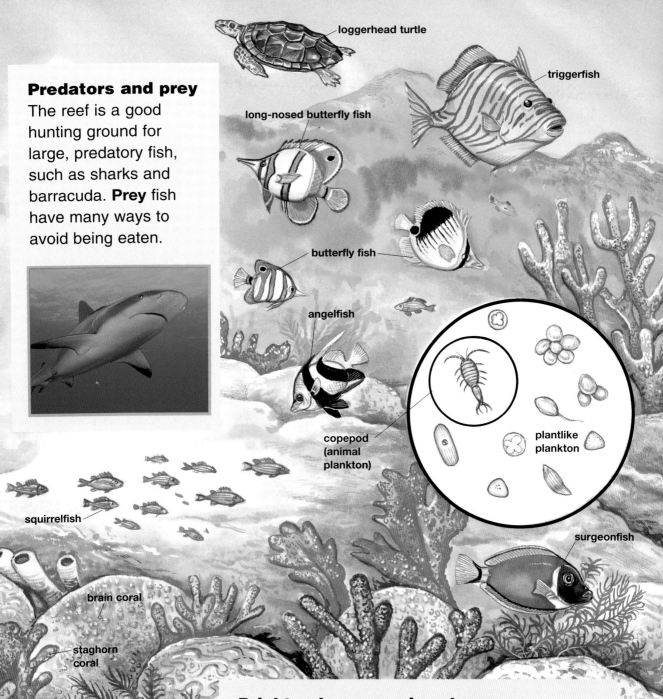

loggerhead turtle

triggerfish

long-nosed butterfly fish

Predators and prey

The reef is a good hunting ground for large, predatory fish, such as sharks and barracuda. **Prey** fish have many ways to avoid being eaten.

butterfly fish

angelfish

copepod (animal plankton)

plantlike plankton

squirrelfish

surgeonfish

brain coral

staghorn coral

Bright colors, amazing shapes

Bright, beautiful fish such as angelfish and surgeon-fish weave their way among waving sea fans and sponges. Their bold stripes and markings blend in with the shadows of the reef.

parrotfish

coral

The coral kingdom

Coral reefs are made of the skeletons of billions of tiny coral polyps. The largest reefs have taken thousands, or millions, of years to form.

▲ *Starfish move around the reef very slowly, holding on with small suckers on the underside of their body.*

▶ *Coral reefs are built by animals called coral polyps. These delicate polyps live only in clear, warm, shallow waters.*

A coral polyp is a small animal with a soft, tube-shaped body. On top of its body is a ring of stinging tentacles. The polyp uses these tentacles to capture tiny floating animals for food. In reef-building corals, the bottom of the polyp's body is not soft but hard and stony.

▶ *Reef-building corals need sunlight to grow. This large, branching elkhorn coral is growing toward the sunlight at the surface of the water.*

8

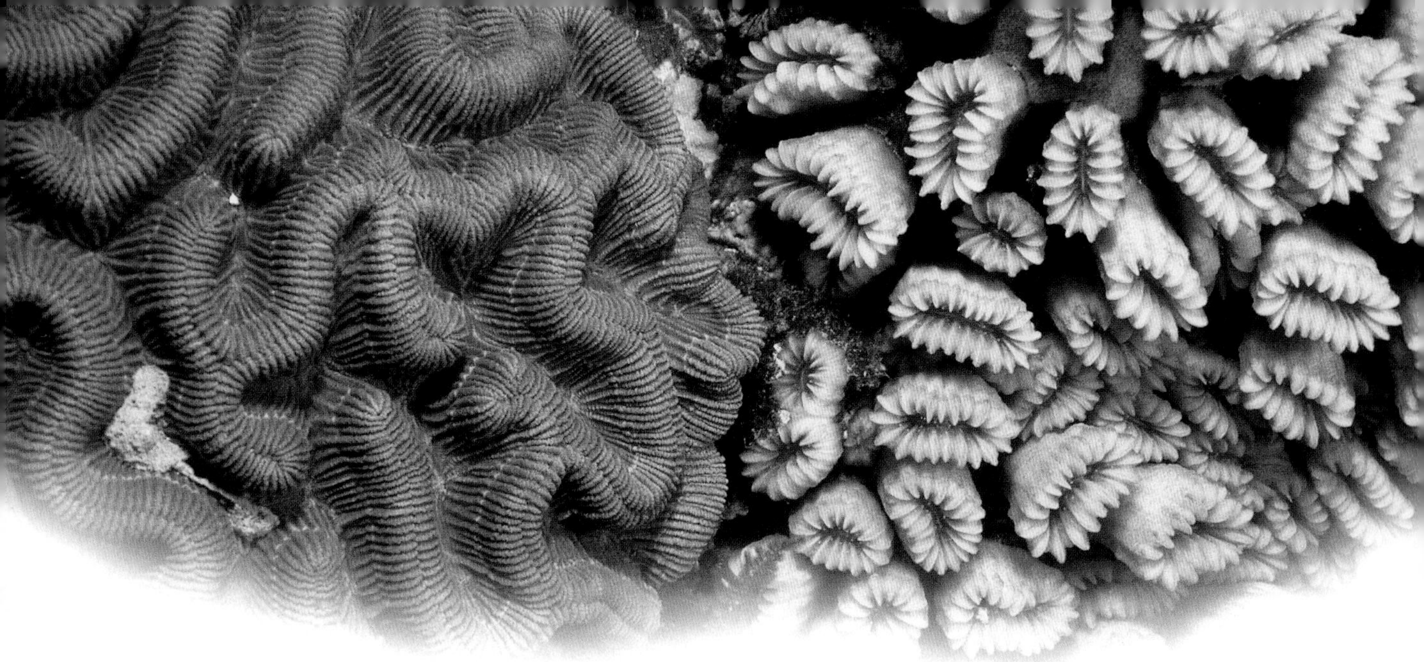

▲ *Many corals are named for their shape. This picture shows brain coral (left) and star coral (right).*

Reef-building corals

Reef-building coral polyps take in calcium bicarbonate from the surrounding seawater. Each polyp then produces a substance called calcium carbonate, which builds a white, cup-shaped shell under the thin layer of flesh on the underside of its body. This hard, and sometimes brittle, chalky shell anchors the polyp to the reef. When the polyp dies, its skeleton remains. Over hundreds of years, the coral reef slowly grows as the polyp skeletons build up, layer upon layer.

FANTASTIC FACTS

- As a reef builds up, the layers of polyp skeletons are gradually crushed. Eventually, they turn into a hard rock called limestone.
- Of the several thousand species of coral, fewer than 1,000 are reef-building stony corals.

Stony and soft corals

There are many different kinds of corals. Some types of hard corals are shaped like saucers or grooved pillars. Brain corals look like a human brain. Only some hard, or stony, corals build coral reefs.

Soft corals and sea fans have delicate orange, yellow, or purple leaflike fronds that sway gently in the ocean currents. Tiny grains of calcium carbonate, called spicules, strengthen the bodies of these corals. Soft corals and sea fans are sometimes shaped like deer antlers or fans.

Coral reef zones

Reefs can be divided into different zones. The reef crest is the highest point of the reef. Many crests are uncovered when the sea draws back during low tide. Behind the crest, between the reef and the shore, lies a **lagoon** of warm, shallow, sunlit water.

▼ *Coral reefs are home to many types of animals. One reef in Key Largo, Florida, has more than 550 different animal species.*

▲ Shrimp make their home on reefs, where they find plenty of microscopic animals to eat.

▼ Christmas tree worms live in burrows in the coral. By extending their spiral fans, the Christmas tree worm can capture food from the water.

On the seaward side, where the crest faces the ocean, the reef slopes down to a depth of 150 feet (45 meters).

The various zones of the reef support different types of marine life. Flatfish, eels, crabs, and sea urchins live on the sandy seabed behind the reef crest. Barnacles and chitons cling to the top of the reef, where they are pounded by waves. Anemones, sponges, fish, snails, clams, and mussels crowd the seaward reef slopes, which drop into deep water. Sharks, barracuda, and other large fish haunt the dark blue waters of the deep reef.

Giant sponges the size of barrels grow in the deep reef. Some reef sponges are large enough for a human diver to swim inside.

Every nook and cranny in the reef shelters a tiny fish, shrimp, eel, crab, worm, or other marine animal. Some reef animals, such as date mussels, burrow into the living coral. Sponges and seaweeds anchor themselves on the reef, helping them stay in place during violent storms.

Filter feeders and browsers

Reef animals include some that stay in one place and those that move very little. Sea anemones are close relatives of coral polyps. They grip the reef with a sticky structure on their base called a pedal disk. Giant clams, oysters, scallops, and mussels also make their home on the reef, where they hold on using a muscular "foot." Most clams and mussels are **filter feeders** and eat by sifting the water for tiny animals.

Starfish, crabs, and sea snails crawl around the coral.

▼ *The tentacles of some sea anemones are armed with stingers to catch prey such as small fish.*

The reef at night

Divers who swim in the sunlit waters of the coral reef by day get to see only some of its wildlife. Many reef animals are nocturnal, or active at night. During the day, sea cucumbers, sea slugs, starfish, and snails (below) lie low in the reef's many cracks and crannies. When night falls, they come out to look for food. Some coral polyps are also nocturnal. In the daytime, these polyps are tightly closed, but at night they open up and spread their tentacles to snare microscopic animals called zooplankton.

These slow-moving animals creep along the reef and search the rocky crevices for food. Some sea urchins, sea slugs, and marine snails such as conches and cowries are vegetarians. They do not eat meat but nibble on algae and seaweed instead. Other reef animals are meat-eating predators. A few others feed on the coral itself.

Coral munchers

Parrotfish eat coral by breaking off pieces of living coral with their beaklike mouth. Then they grind up the hard, chalky parts of the polyps to get a type of **algae** called zooxanthellae from inside. Some starfish also feed on living coral. They crawl over the reef, releasing chemicals that dissolve the polyps' bodies. The dissolved bodies make a polyp soup that the starfish eat. In the Pacific and Indian Oceans, giant crown-of-thorns starfish prey on the reefs. These spiny animals swarm over the coral, eating and leaving behind large, bare patches.

FANTASTIC FACTS
● Reef-building corals depend on tiny plantlike algae called zooxanthellae, which live inside the polyps. The algae provide the polyps with food and oxygen.
● Reef-building corals cannot live in deep seas because the zooxanthellae thrive only in shallow, sunlit waters.

▼ *Parrotfish have sharp teeth at the front of their mouth to break off pieces of coral. Another set of teeth farther back in their throat grind the hard coral.*

Bright colors, amazing shapes

Reef animals come in strange shapes and all the colors of the rainbow. For some animals, their bright patterns act as a warning to predators.

▲ *A flame scallop on a Florida Keys reef. It has tiny eyes on the shorter stalks that fringe its shell.*

▶ *Seahorses use their tail as an anchor when they feed. They wrap it around corals and underwater grasses, or even around each other.*

The fish of the reef have many different shapes. Most fish have a tapering, streamlined body, so they move easily through the water. Seahorses have an unusual shape, with a head like that of a horse and a long, curling tail like that of a monkey. Angelfish are tall and narrow.

▶ *Like beautiful birds flying among the trees in a rainforest, these brightly colored fish weave in and out of pillar coral on a reef.*

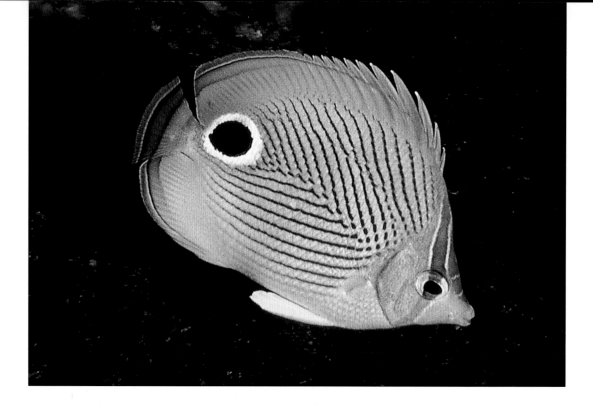

▲ *In this picture of a butterfly fish you can see its slender snout and the dark eyespot near its tail.*

Angelfish are difficult to see from the front, which helps them swim up to their prey without being detected. Pipefish and trumpet fish are long and slender and can hide among the seagrass, where they swim with their head hanging down. Flounders have a wide, flat body so they can swim along the seabed. Butterfly fish use their keen eyesight to look for food in the holes and cracks of the reef.

Spots and stripes

Many animals on coral reefs have colored patterns or bold markings on their bodies. These markings can warn predators not to eat them because they taste bad or are even poisonous.

Other body markings help animals **camouflage** themselves by blending in with their surroundings so they cannot be seen easily.

Some butterfly fish have dark spots called eyespots near their tails, which look like eyes. These markings can fool enemies into attacking the wrong end of the fish, allowing it to escape.

▼ Sergeant major fish get their name because their markings are similar to the five black stripes on the badge of a sergeant major in the army.

Many fish have bold stripes running vertically or horizontally along their body. These markings break up their body outline, helping them hide among corals and seaweeds. In the open water, these same markings make the fish stand out clearly. This is useful during the breeding season, when the fish try to attract others of the same species. They swim out in the open water to attract their mates and to frighten rival fish away.

FANTASTIC FACTS

- Coral colonies grow slowly—adding only about half an inch (1 centimeter) a year.
- Some coral reefs are 40–50 million years old. These reefs are made up of coral three-quarters of a mile (1.2 kilometers) thick.

Male and female

The males and females of some fish are different colors. For example, in one type of parrotfish, males are green, while females are black, white, and red. They look so different from each other that scientists once thought the fish belonged to separate species. The colors make it easy for the parrotfish to find mates.

Young and old

In some angelfish, the young and adult fish are colored differently. Young queen angelfish are dark blue with pale stripes that blend in with the ocean's ripples. Adults are bright blue with flecks of gold. Young angelfish have protective camouflage, but the adults are more obvious in open water. These fish pair for life, and set up breeding **territories** on the reef, which they defend against rivals. The adults swim into the open to scare other angelfish off their coral patch.

▼ *Like queen angelfish, French angelfish do not look the same throughout their life. Here you can see a young (left) and an adult (right) French angelfish.*

Changing color

Bottom-dwelling fish such as flounders have mottled colors that blend in with the ocean floor. They can slowly change color as they move from rock to sand. Cuttlefish can change color quickly, turning from brown to beige, orange, or green in an instant. Their bodies ripple with color as they creep along the bottom in search of food.

▼ *Octopuses are related to cuttlefish and squid. They can match their color very closely to that of the rocky reef.*

Living together

In the crowded waters of the reef, some animals make unusual partnerships with other animal species. Like the coral and its live-in guests, the zooxanthellae, these animals depend on one another for shelter, food, and protection.

Cleaning service

On some coral reefs, small fish called cleaner wrasse provide an amazing service for larger fish. They nibble **parasites** that infest the body of their "clients." The larger fish recognize the cleaners and allow them to approach and feed unharmed and even swim inside their mouth to search for parasites. Both partners benefit from this relationship—the wrasse get a free meal, and the client fish is rid of pesky parasites. Sometimes the larger fish line up patiently at a wrasse's cleaning station until the smaller fish is ready to clean.

Many cleaner wrasse have bright stripes running along or down their bodies. These stripes help distinguish them from other fish. Other fish called false cleaners have similar patterns. They fool the client fish into letting them approach, then they bite the big fish and swim away!

Partnerships that benefit two organisms equally are called mutualisms. Relationships that benefit only one organism in the partnership are called parasitisms.

Give and take

Anemone fish, or clown fish, are brightly colored fish that live among the stinging tentacles of sea anemones. The tentacles are venomous and can paralyze other fish, but the clown fish is covered with slimy mucus, which protects it from the stings. The clown fish lives and rears its young among the waving tentacles, safe from predators. In return, it provides food for the anemone by tempting other fish within reach of the tentacles.

Some partnerships benefit only one species, while the other species is unaffected. The pearl fish is a slim, transparent fish that lives inside the partly hollow body of certain sea cucumbers, which are relatives of the starfish. The little pearl fish gains a protective shelter and also nibbles at its host's insides. The sea cucumber quickly regrows the nibbled parts and does not seem bothered by its guest's eating habits.

FANTASTIC FACTS
● Living coral reefs cover 360,000 square miles (930,000 square kilometers) of the world's oceans—an area the size of Texas and Colorado.
● Scientists believe that the Florida Keys reefs formed 125,000 years ago, during a time known as the Pleistocene Age.

◀ *A remora is attached to the lower jaw of this shark by a sucker on the top of its head. Remoras attach themselves for a free ride, at times eating scraps of their host's meals.*

Predators and prey

The reef is a dangerous world, where the rule is "eat and be eaten." Both predators and prey have tricks for survival.

▲ *Barracuda have excellent eyesight and are fierce hunters on Florida's coral reefs.*

▶ *The whale shark is the largest fish in the world. It filters plankton, small fish, and other animals from the water as it swims along.*

Some animals on the coral reef are herbivores, or plant eaters, that eat algae and seagrass. Many are carnivores, or meat eaters. Some feed on **carrion** and do not catch live prey. They are known as scavengers. Usually, the smallest animals of the reef are eaten by medium-size hunters, which fall prey to larger **predators**.

▶ *As these fish turn through the water, light reflects off their scales. This confuses predators and makes the fish difficult to catch.*

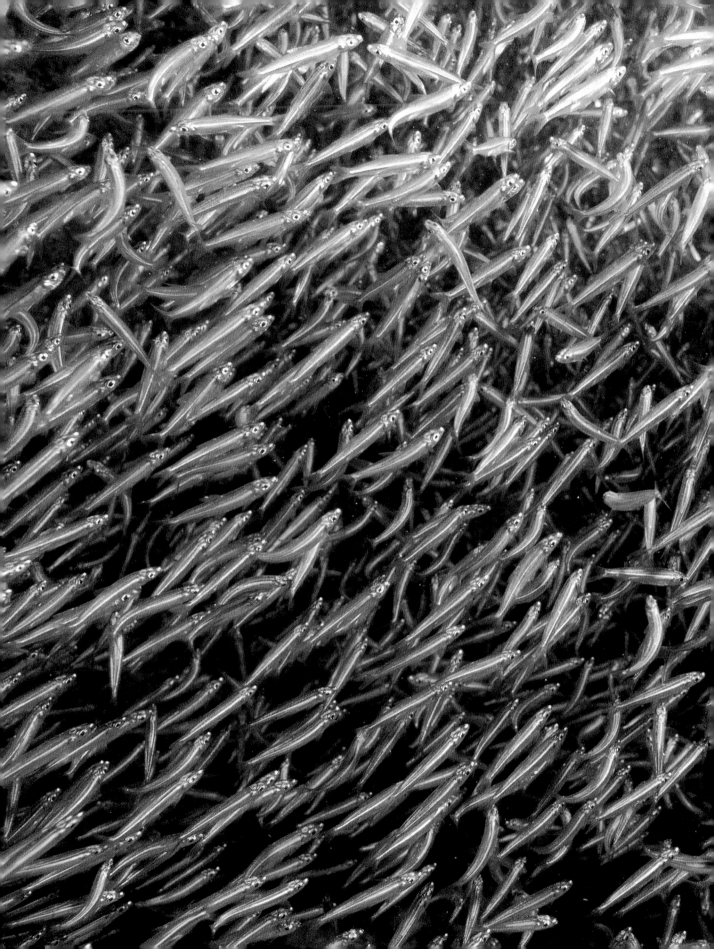

plantlike plankton

copepod

There are some exceptions to this rule. For example, the whale shark feeds on tiny shrimp and fish. A food web shows the relationships that link the animals of the reef. A food web is made up of several food chains.

shrimp

barracuda

▲ *A coral reef food chain. Little, invisible plankton are the base of this food chain. Tiny copepods feed on the plankton; shrimp eat the copepods; angelfish eat the shrimp; and larger fish eat the smaller fish.*

angelfish

shark

FANTASTIC FACTS

● The mouth of a whale shark may be more than four feet (1.2 meters) wide.

● Barracuda are sometimes called the "tigers of the sea" because they are ferocious predators.

● Like octopuses, some groupers can change their color to blend in with the background.

Top hunters

At the top of each reef food chain are large predatory fish such as groupers. Hunters of the open ocean, including dolphins, tuna, marlin, and sailfish, also patrol the deep waters off the reef. Barracuda are common on reefs. They are giant fish up to 12 feet (3.5 meters) long, with razor-sharp teeth.

Barracuda sometimes follow human divers, but they rarely attack.

Sharks are predators that swim in all oceans. Mako and tiger sharks have sometimes attacked people, but most sharks are harmless to humans. Hammerhead sharks are among the strangest-looking fish in the oceans. Their eyes and nostrils are mounted on large, fleshy projections that form a giant "T." Scientists believe this helps them track their prey.

A shark's main weapon is its sharp teeth, used for gripping slippery fish and slicing through flesh. Other predators have more unusual weapons. Some rays and eels can generate an electric current to stun their prey, which they then snap up in their jaws.

▲ *Tiger groupers feed on smaller fish, gripping them with their needlelike teeth. In turn, they fall prey to sharks and barracuda.*

▼ *Green moray eels hide away in cracks and holes in the reef, waiting for their prey. This one is being cleaned by a shrimp.*

Reefs in danger

Coral reefs like those on the Florida Keys face many threats to their survival. Some of these threats are natural, but many are caused by humans. Stocks of some reef fish have dwindled due to overfishing, which upsets the natural balance of the food webs. Sewage from cities, oil spills, and chemicals from farms and factories pollute the reef waters. Some chemicals cause algae to multiply, threatening to smother the reef and use up the oxygen. Pollution also makes the coral polyps open to disease.

Storms and rough seas sometimes smash the coral. Divers and snorkelers also do harm when they walk on or scrape against the delicate coral, or break off pieces to take home as souvenirs. Coral reefs now face a new danger: global warming. Global warming is the increase in the temperature of Earth's atmosphere that many scientists believe will threaten whole areas of coral reef. Polyps and their live-in algae are very sensitive to temperature changes in the water around them.

Although many dangers threaten coral reefs, people are trying to save them. Large areas of reef are now protected as national parks. Scientists monitor the waters for **pollution**. Park rules help protect the reef from damage by tourists. In 1960, the area of Key Largo was protected when the first U.S. marine park, John Pennekamp State Park, was established.

Escaping danger

Prey fish and other animals of the coral reef have many ways of avoiding danger. Fish such as herring and grunts swim in large groups called schools. These groups provide safety in numbers. As the whole school twists and turns as a glittering mass, a predator finds it difficult to single out individual fish to attack.

Many coral reef-dwellers have camouflage colors that disguise them from predators. Others have bright colors and striking patterns to warn predators to keep away. Some, such as soap fish, are poisonous or taste bad. Predators that try to eat them soon spit them out! Surgeonfish and triggerfish are armed with sharp spines that ward off attackers. Starfish can regrow their arms if predators eat them. Hermit crabs hide their soft body inside sturdy empty shells that once belonged to other marine animals, such as snails.

FANTASTIC FACTS

● Florida Keys Marine Park was enlarged in 1981, and again in 1989. Now it stretches 220 miles (350 kilometers) from Biscayne in the northeast to Dry Tortugas in the west.

● Around 2.5 million tourists visit Florida Keys Marine Park each year.

▼ *This sea slug is squirting ink into the water to confuse predators, giving it time to escape.*

Getting to know reefs

The Florida Keys may be far from where you live, but you can see reef animals in aquariums. The nearest seashore also has species similar to those on reefs.

▲ *Snorkeling on coral reefs is exciting, but reefs are fragile. When you snorkel, be careful not to damage the reef or disturb its inhabitants.*

If you live in the southeastern United States, the reefs may be on your doorstep. The coral kingdom is yours to explore with just a snorkel and diving mask. Always take an adult with you when you swim.

Elsewhere in North America, visit your local aquarium or sea life center to see reef animals in homes that are similar to their natural habitats. Look up sea life and marine park websites to find out more about the animals of the coral reef.

Sandy and rocky seashores and river **estuaries** are home to animals closely related to coral reef species. Your next trip to the seashore can become a wildlife expedition! Look for anemones, small fish, crabs, and starfish in tidal pools. Mollusks such as limpets and mussels cling to wave-soaked rocks on the shore.

▶ *Many aquariums have "touch pools." These let you see and feel some of the animals that live in tidal pools and on coral reefs without going to the coast or venturing under water!*

Shrimp, crabs, and worms hide in the sand or under stones on the beach. Take a notepad with you and record the animals that you see.

Place your finds in a bucket of seawater while you study them. A magnifying glass will make it easier to see them. When you have finished, put the animals back where you found them. You can also search the beach for the remains of marine animals, such as empty shells.

TOP TIPS FOR BEACH DETECTIVES

1 Rocks on the seashore are often very slippery. Be careful as you move around. Store your possessions in a backpack to leave both hands free to grip the rocks.

2 When exploring tidal pools, place a diver's facemask on the surface of the water to see more clearly.

3 Be careful not to touch sea urchins or stranded jellyfish. These animals can give you a painful sting.

Words to know

algae Tiny plantlike organisms.

camouflage Colors and patterns that help an animal blend in with its surroundings.

carrion Dead meat.

estuary The part of a river where the current and tide meet.

filter feeder An animal that sifts water for algae or animals to eat.

lagoon An area of calm water between reef crest and shore.

parasite An organism that takes food or shelter from its host and usually harms it in return.

pollution Harmful substances in the air, water, or soil.

polyps A small water animal with a tube-shaped body and tentacles.

predator An animal that hunts other animals for food.

prey An animal that is eaten by another animal.

species A group of plants or animals that are similar and are able to mate and have offspring.

territory A breeding or feeding area that an animal defends against other animals.

Index

anemone fish 23

angelfish 16, 20–18

barracuda 24, 26

brain coral 10

butterfly fish 18, 19

Christmas tree worm 12

clam 16, 13

cleaner wrasse 22

common octopus 21

coral polyp 8, 10

cuttlefish 21

elkhorn coral 8, 9

flame scallop 16

green moray eel 27

mussel 13

parrotfish 15, 20

pillar coral 16, 17

remora 23

sea anemone 13

sea fan 11

seahorse 16

sea slug 14, 15, 29

sergeant major fish 19

shark 7, 23

shrimp 12, 27

soft coral 11

sponge 4, 13

star coral 10

starfish 8, 15, 29

stony coral 10

tiger grouper 27

whale shark 24, 26

zooxanthellae 14, 15